WINDOWS OF WORSHIP™

REAL LIFE REFLECTIONS

Gifts of Friendship

PAUL S. WILLIAMS, *Editor*

Stories for Spiritual Growth

Standard
PUBLISHING
Bringing The Word to Life™

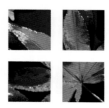

© 2005 CNI Holdings Corp., Windows of Worship is a Trademark of
Christian Network, Inc.

Published by Standard Publishing, Cincinnati, Ohio. A division of Standex
International Corporation. Printed in China.

Edited by: Paul S. Williams
Content editor: Molly Detweiler
Art direction and design: Rule29
Cover design: Rule29 | rule29.com

ISBN 0-7847-1662-5

11 10 09 08 07 06 05   9 8 7 6 5 4 3 2 1

He made it simple . . .

God didn't give us 10,000 different rules to follow. We don't
even have to worry about the 613 laws of the Old Testament—
set out for a different age. No, as Christians we have just one
responsibility. To live like Christ, reflecting him in our lives.
I said he made it simple. I did not say it was easy!

So how do we do it? Jesus' answer was simple: Love God
with all your heart, soul, and mind, and love your neighbor
as yourself.

That is our challenge, to love God with everything we have, and
to love our neighbors likewise. My hope is that, as you read
these reflections from the lives of people who have answered
that challenge, you will be encouraged to do the same. Keep it
simple: live a real life, reflecting a very real God.

PAUL S. WILLIAMS
Chairman of the Board of Stewards
The Christian Network, Inc.

Confess your sins to each other and pray for each other so that you may be healed.

James 5:16

Telling Secrets

When my son was about 4 years old he went with his mother to pick out my Christmas present. All the way home his mom told him, "Now you have to keep this a secret. You can't tell Daddy what we got him for Christmas." Jonathan promised his mother, "I won't."

They hadn't been home half an hour when Jonathan said, "Hey, Daddy, we got your Christmas present.

It's a coat." Cathy, my wife, said, "Jonathan, you were supposed to keep that a secret." He protested, "But, Mommy, I didn't tell him it was blue." So much for keeping secrets.

Lots of folks have a difficult time keeping secrets. But it's not failing to keep secrets that I'm talking about today. It's finding the courage to tell them.

One of Frederick Buechner's autobiographical works is entitled *Telling Secrets*. I like that title. We all have secrets—thoughts, memories, feelings we keep to ourselves. These are secrets we are not inclined to tell. They seem too terrible. We think, *If people knew that, they would not love me*. And these untold secrets can do us much harm. They can lead to guilt, shame, depression, or worse.

One of the most important things we can do with our secrets is share them in a safe place. Think of someone you've known a long time, someone not inclined to say, "But I didn't tell him it was blue." Find someone who can keep a confidence, probably someone older than you, with the wisdom of having fallen off the bike a time or two in life, with the scrapes and scars to show for it. It might be a professional counselor. That's usually a safe place to start. But it might be an ordinary citizen as well, someone who seems on a journey similar to yours, someone widely respected by others.

Find such a person and tell him or her your secrets. Bring the secrets to light, where you can look at them with the other person. You will quickly discover you are not alone with your secrets, and that you have far more company than you thought. You will find many of the things you fear and the failings you hide are common to others as well. In so doing, trusting friends will love you more deeply and more intimately than before. And you will no longer be anchored with the terrible burden of a hidden thought, untold.

Opening up about our innermost fears, desires, hopes, dreams, horrible memories, and personal failings not only heals those hurts, it also creates community and a deeper bond with others. As a result of our honesty, others will realize they are not alone. They may even have had similar feelings they were afraid to express. But now, with the courage you've shown, they too can find the courage to speak the thoughts they've kept hidden.

Confession is good for the soul. If you are a Christian, God has already forgiven you for even the deepest and darkest of your secrets. In sharing your pain with another person, maybe finally you can forgive yourself.

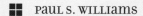 PAUL S. WILLIAMS

Who has been brave enough to share secrets with you?
How did you feel to be considered a trustworthy friend
in that way?

Take a first step in revealing your secrets by writing
them down here. Write a prayer about those secrets,
asking God to guide you to a trustworthy confidant.

If anyone has caused grief . . . you ought to forgive and comfort him, so that he will not be overwhelmed by excessive sorrow. I urge you, therefore, to reaffirm your love for him.

2 Corinthians 2:5, 7, 8

Hope for Peter

I don't really *want* to tell you this story, but I think I *need* to tell it to you. Years ago I really disappointed a friend, Bob, who is also my boss. He is very good at what he does, maybe one of the best there is. But some years ago I had watched another excellent leader too—his name was Bill. So I thought I'd challenge my boss to adopt some of Bill's style. More accurately I'd have to say that I was arrogantly critical of Bob and, in my immaturity, told him he could better himself and our team if he'd only see the wisdom of another style. The sad part of my pitiful mistake is that I didn't even know how deeply I had hurt my friend until about a month ago.

We were reminiscing about those good old days, and as I admitted my mistake, Bob looked up and said, "You really hurt me then." Now *I* was devastated. I committed the crime years ago but was feeling the pain now. I turned to Bob and said, "I'm really sorry." He smiled and said, "Oh, you're forgiven—I forgave you a long time ago." And that, my friends, is what happens in a deep and abiding friendship.

I deeply hurt my friend Bob with my damaging words. The apostle Peter did the very same thing— to Jesus! When the whole world was ready to kill Jesus, you'd think his closest friends would stand by him. But the fear of being killed right along with Jesus caused even his closest friends, like Peter, to abandon him. As a matter of fact, while Jesus was being taken away to be crucified, three different people asked if Peter was a friend of Jesus and all three times Peter angrily protested, "No, I don't know the man."

Then, Peter heard a rooster crow in the distance and felt the pain deep inside. Peter remembered that Jesus had predicted he would deny their friendship three times before the rooster crowed in the morning. Hours later, Jesus was killed. Now how could there be hope for forgiveness after a betrayal like that?

But three days later Jesus came back from the dead and appeared to a few people, including Peter. Just as Peter had denied their friendship three times, Jesus asked Peter "Do you love me?" three times.

And in that simple gesture, Jesus gave Peter the hope of forgiveness and restoration.

Jesus knew that I would hurt Bob even before I opened my immature mouth that dreadful day. And Jesus knew the same about Peter. Jesus also knew that there was hope for all thoughtlessly spoken words and the people who spoke them. That hope is in the forgiveness offered by good friends—a forgiveness born in the heart of Jesus.

Greg Allen

What were your feelings when someone forgave you for hurting them? How do you think the other person felt?

How did your friendship change after you had weathered a time of hurt and betrayal together? Is there someone you need to forgive today?

Encourage one another daily, as long as it is called Today.

HEBREWS 3:13

White Combs and Sweet Honey

Last summer I needed to replace the blade on my hedge trimmer. But when three trips to three stores found no blades, I simply bought a new hedge trimmer for $29.95. I threw the old one away. After all, I'm a busy man. I can't be bothered with goods that are slightly damaged. Sadly, I sometimes find myself tempted to do the same thing with people.

Suppose I have a friend who struggles with depression. Do I really want to devote the time necessary to hang on through his far-too-frequent dark nights? Or would it be easier to disengage from the friendship? After all, how many people can I help through their significant problems? I have a wife and three kids.

But when I dismiss a person because of obvious wounds, I'm ignoring the person's underlying gifts. Often friends and loved ones have had to travel through my wounds to get to my gifts. What gives me the right to ignore the hidden gifts of others?

I have a friend who is the president of a sizable corporation. He won't hire anyone for a leadership position unless he knows the person has been broken. To quote him: "Until you fall off the bike once or twice, you don't know much of anything." I like his approach. I've fallen off the bike a lot. And in my own life I have found my failures to be far more instructive than my successes. David Whyte in *The Heart Aroused* can resonate with the Spanish poet Antonio Machado who wrote, "Last night, as I was sleeping, I dreamt—marvelous error!—that I had a beehive here inside my heart. And the golden bees were making white combs and sweet honey from my old failures."

Sometimes it works out that way, but not always. Sometimes my failures have buried me in shame and guilt and loss. I've come to learn that when I fail alone and isolated, I don't crawl out of the muck so well. Sweet honey only comes from my old failures when someone has taken the time to love me through them. And through the loving touch of that caring human being, I am healed.

God's been in the business of creating sweet honey for a long time. He chose a former murderer who couldn't speak in public—Moses—to lead his people through the wilderness. He took a man who committed adultery and then committed murder to cover it up, and not only made him a king, but made him a man after his own heart. That king was David. Imagine that—a murderer being called a man after God's own heart! Now that's creating white combs and sweet honey from old failures.

Every last one of us is broken. God gave freely of himself to look past my broken side and see my possibilities. That ought to give me courage to do the same for others. So when a friend of mine hits the deep dark night, I hope I won't bail on him. I hope I'll stick around through his pain, so that together we can make white combs and sweet honey from old failures.

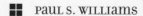 PAUL S. WILLIAMS

Have you been tempted to "throw away" friends or
family members because of their brokenness?
Have you ever been discarded by someone while in
the midst of your struggles?

Have you ever helped make "honey" out of someone's
failures? Has someone done the same for you? What was
the outcome?

God created man in his own image,
in the image of God he created him;
male and female he created them.

GENESIS 1:27

The Most Beautiful
Part of Creation

In his book, *Contemplation to Attain the Love of God*,
Ignatius of Loyola, the sixteenth-century founder
of the Jesuits, urged readers to see how God's glory
dwells in all of his creation—in the elements, in the
plants, and in the animals.

But Ignatius concluded that the most amazing work
of God was not in the plants or animals. The most

amazing work of God was in humanity. And he said so in these words: "So he dwells in me and gives me being, life, sensation, intelligence; and makes a temple of me, since I am created in the likeness and image of the Divine Majesty."

The most beautiful part of creation has always been people—those made in the image of the almighty God. The crowning achievement of God's creation was man. And the most remarkable of human beings was God himself in human form—Jesus Christ.

After Jesus was resurrected from the dead, his friends often did not recognize him. Once he was mistaken for a gardener. Another time, on the road to Emmaus, he was mistaken for a lonely traveler, maybe even a vagabond. On the shore of Galilee, offering free advice about where to fish, he was an unknown bystander.

I always took that lack of recognition to be the unwillingness of those encountering Jesus to see the resurrected Lord who was clearly in front of their eyes. But maybe that's not the case.

Maybe it was Jesus who was making himself difficult to be seen, teaching his friends that he would be with them always, as he promised, but in ways far more subtle than they might have liked. Perhaps he was teaching them that he would be with them in the world at large and in the faces of strangers.

I've never seen the face of God. Moses saw the back of God. I've never seen that either. But I do think I've seen God's shadow. When I gaze upon nature I see the work of God. But when I gaze into the eyes of those I love and those who love me, I think I see more than the work of God. I see his shadow—his shadow alive in the eyes of the beloved.

It was the apostle John who said that it's not that God looks like love, or that God loves, but that God *is* love. The next time you look into the eyes of someone you love, look deeply and see if you can see the shadow of God there.

PAUL S. WILLIAMS

In whom do you see the "shadow of God"?
What about this person speaks to you of the beauty
of the Lord?

Do you think others can see God in you?
In what practical, specific ways can you show the love
of God to others so that they might see his shadow in
your eyes?

Dear friends, since God so loved us, we also ought to love one another. No one has seen God; but if we love one another, God lives in us and his love is made complete in us.

1 JOHN 4:11, 12

God's Got Skin

On the occasion of the 19th birthday of my friend's second child, she wrote a story for her.

It was a beautiful summer Sunday. July, I think. The family was beginning our week-at-the-beach vacation. The girls were young then, eager to go, happy to be together. It was a good day, I'm sure, though I don't remember much about the specifics. Certainly there must have been playing in the sand—pails, shovels, cartwheels down the sand cliff, swimming in the ocean! What great fun!

We didn't go to church that day. But, trying to instill in the children a sense that with all of our busyness we still do not take a vacation from God, I thought I'd have a special prayer service for the girls, to direct their thoughts to Jesus, to be thankful for what they had. It seemed only fitting.

Before bedtime the girls, my husband, and I gathered around the table. We lit a candle, read from Scripture, and said some prayers. Bethany, our middle girl, kept beseeching, "Can I blow out the candle? Can I blow out the candle?" Once we had finished I said, "Yes, Bethany, you can blow out the candle." It was a fine end to a wonderful day. . . .

The next night the girls were again ready for bed when Bethany pleaded, "Can we pray with the candle?" Her father looked at me with one of those Now-look-what-you've-started looks, but we again gathered around the table and prayed. Again I told them,

"The candle reminds us that Jesus is with us. Even if we blow out the candle, he is still here." Bethany, pursing her lips, said, "Jesus is always with me? Like, if I be scared, then Jesus is with me."

"That's right, Beth," I affirmed, pleased that she had learned a profound theological truth. Bethany thought a little longer. "But if I be really, really scared, Mommy, would you climb in bed with me too?"

What a perfect illustration of the incarnation. We can experience God with us in a beautiful cathedral or a towering mountain range. But the other experience of God with us, the experience that touches us in the deepest parts of our souls, is in things like the warm hug of a loving mother on a scary night.

God came to Earth once and lived for 33 years. That was good because we are creatures of the senses who needed a God who has skin. But after a short time on Earth, God was gone, returned to Heaven, and no one has felt the physical embrace of God since. Or have they?

Maybe in her childlike faith Bethany caught a glimpse of a greater truth. God does have skin on Earth even now—in the form of her mother, Florence—a mother in whom Christ abides. We who are followers of God are his skin. And we are called on to climb into bed now and again to comfort God's frightened children. We should take seriously the words of Teresa of Avila:

Christ has no body now but yours,
No hands but yours,
No feet but yours,
Yours are the eyes through which Christ's compassion
must look out on the world.
Yours are the feet with which he is to go about doing good.
Yours are the hands with which he is to bless us now.

 PAUL S. WILLIAMS

Who has been "God with skin on" for you?
How did they show you God's love in tangible ways?

Who needs you to be "God with skin on" for them?
What can you do to touch them with God's love?

Who may ascend the hill of the L<small>ORD</small>?

Who may stand in his holy place?

He who has clean hands and a pure heart. . . .

He will receive blessing from the L<small>ORD</small>.

PSALM 24:1-6

Amazing Grace

It has been my privilege to serve on the board of
directors of a nonprofit company that operates
homes for individuals with developmental disabilities. I have been wonderfully impressed with
the people who provide care for the residents of
those homes. They are marvelous caregivers who
are deeply concerned about each resident. There is
grounding in that kind of service, whether it is paid
or volunteer, that provides wisdom.

Henri Nouwen, the former Harvard and Yale professor, learned this when he went to work with the Daybreak Community in Toronto, Canada. He received from the residents there a love and acceptance that he had never known before.

Maybe that is why thousands of people, for centuries, have called those with developmental disabilities "children of God."

A church in West Virginia warmly invites residents from a home similar to Daybreak to participate in their church services. On one occasion the workers took several residents, including one whose religious background was unknown, to a spiritual retreat. When the workers were ready to depart, shortly before the congregants celebrated the Lord's Supper, one particular resident of the group home refused to leave. When the time came to receive Communion, she insisted on joining in.

She didn't talk much, but she obviously understood the Lord's Supper, and she wanted to participate.

The church and the home worked together to disciple this woman, and she later joined the church. Though she rarely spoke at all, on the day that she was welcomed as a member she stood at the front of the church and began to sing. That's right. She began to sing—"Amazing grace, how sweet the sound, that saved a wretch like me. I once was lost, but now I'm found, was blind, but now I see."

That particular woman may in fact have a developmental disability, but there is no mistaking that she understands life's most important truth. The workers, volunteers, and others joined in the song and realized they were all, every last one of them, children of God, privileged to ascend the hill of the Lord and stand in a holy place, with clean hands and pure heart.

In the hills of West Virginia, at a generous church, and in the living room of a home of eight individuals, who just happen to have developmental disabilities, God is known. And he invites *all* who will come to ascend the hill of the Lord.

PAUL S. WILLIAMS

When you come across someone with a physical or mental disability, what is your first reaction? Why do you think you react this way?

Because of sin, we are all disabled spiritually, if not physically or mentally. How does that idea change your thoughts about those with outward disabilities? How does it make you feel to know that God's grace makes us all whole again, no matter what our challenges?

Always be prepared to give an answer to everyone who asks you to give the reason for the hope that you have. But do this with gentleness and respect.

1 Peter 3:15

Nic at Night

Gary manages a great little barbecue place with red-checkered tablecloths, a concrete floor, and the absolute best sweet tea. Over time Gary and I have talked enough for him to know that I work at a church and for me to know that he doesn't attend church.

But Gary does have a lot of questions—questions like, "So did God cause the terrorist attacks on

New York and D.C.?" As I was lunching on ribs and corn one day Gary said, "I'm 47 years old, and I feel like I'm on a fence, and I have to know what to believe."

Though Gary is a fun guy with a happy outlook, he still wants to know what life's all about. I can hear in his voice and see in his face that he is looking for what all of us are looking for—hope.

Where was God in the terrorist tragedy? In fact, where is God at all? Can you prove I'm not just a cosmic accident? Can you give me hope?

Even fun people who have positive personalities want to know if there is more—if there is more to life than great barbecue and sweet tea. Jobs crash and family members die with one hijacked airplane. The question is, is there hope for more than this world offers?

That's exactly what Nic wanted to know. Nicodemus was the Gary of the first century. He had a lot of questions about God. But he took his questions straight to the source—Jesus.

One night, when his disapproving peers wouldn't see him, Nic found Jesus and quizzed him. He asked really good questions and made it obvious he was just a man sitting on a fence who needed to know what to believe, just like Gary. Jesus told him, "God so loved the world that he gave his one and only Son, that whoever believes in him shall not perish but have eternal life" (John 3:16). There was Nic's hope. There is Gary's hope. And there is your hope.

Gary is still asking questions. I'm glad. Gary's asking questions about God tells me he has not dropped into apathetic indifference. He knows he needs to get off that fence. Maybe you too are on a fence about God. You're just trying to figure this life out. Well, my friend, I'd like to encourage you. Like Nic and Gary, go ahead and ask the hard questions. God can handle them. It's OK to be sitting on a fence for a spell. But I've got a feeling that, if you ask those questions with all your heart, you won't be on the fence for long.

■ GreG ALLen

Who do you know who is still "on the fence" about God?
What are some of the questions they have asked or
doubts they have expressed?

What have you been doing or can you do in the future to
gently guide this person in their journey toward God?
Write a prayer asking for God's special wisdom as you
talk with this person.

Be completely humble and gentle; be patient, bearing with one another in love. Make every effort to keep the unity of the Spirit through the bond of peace. There is one body and one Spirit—just as you were called to one hope when you were called.

EPHESIANS 4:2-4

A Kingdom of Relationships

They say the three jobs of a corporate CEO are vision, financing, and succession. Where is the company going? How are we going to pay for it? And who will take my place when I'm gone?

I wonder if Jesus ever asked those questions. After his resurrection, when he was ready to return to Heaven, from all appearances it looked like his work was done. His followers understood the vision. They were willing to pay for it, with their own lives if necessary. And those same followers, aided by his own Spirit, would take his place when he was gone. Everything was set for the future of Christ's church.

Or was it?

Jesus' followers had seen him, alive and resurrected, after his crucifixion. They saw with their own eyes. Now they were ready for Jesus to become king, to take over the world and run it as it ought to be run. No one would get in his way. Not in Jerusalem. Not in Israel. Not anywhere. He would rule the universe, and his followers would be his political appointees.

But there was someone who stood in the way of those desires, someone who had no interest in political rule. That someone was Jesus himself.

Jesus didn't come to be an earthly king, but it was always difficult for his followers to understand that. They wanted him to defeat his enemies and bring about a new government. And they wanted to have powerful positions within that government. But Jesus had a different idea.

After Jesus' resurrection, his followers gathered with him outside the city of Jerusalem. Jesus told them he was leaving. But they interrupted to ask him one more question. "Is it time now?" they said. "Is it time now for you to create a political kingdom?" They wanted it so badly they could taste it.

I can just see Jesus turning up to the heavens and announcing to the angels waiting to take him home—"Sorry, folks, this'll take just one more minute." And then he turned to his followers and said one last time that his kingdom was not about politics or power. His kingdom was about something else. It was about relationships.

Jesus didn't come to take over the world as political ruler. He came to teach the people of the world how to love one another. He came to establish a kingdom, all right—a kingdom of relationships, built on loving God and loving each other. And when the followers of Jesus finally understood that, then they were ready to start the church that would bear the name of Christ. And Jesus was ready to head back home, his work on Earth finally done.

■■ PAUL S. WILLIAMS

Is your church family working to further God's kingdom by loving others and loving God, or is it trying to
use politics and causes instead? What practical steps
can you take to help your church become a "kingdom of
relationships"?

How can you live your life as a relationship builder?
Write a prayer asking for God's help in becoming a person who nurtures godly community in your world.

[Jesus said,] "For where two or three come together in my name, there am I with them."

MATTHEW 18:20

The Neighborhood Church

I was 4 when we moved out of the city of Syracuse, New York, and into the suburbs of Liverpool, New York, to Green Acres Drive. It was a great neighborhood to grow up in. The street seemed so much bigger then. Everything seemed bigger then.

A few years after we moved onto that street, a church was built on the corner. Our family didn't attend church very often. We went on Easter and

never missed at Christmas. The minister at the new
church was a kind and gracious man who stopped
by our home a few times and invited us to attend,
but we weren't interested.

I did, though, spend a lot of time there. The
churchyard was the biggest lot around. We played
football and baseball games there. The minister
came out sometimes to watch, sometimes to play,
and often just to break up arguments. He was sur-
prisingly normal. He had kids, he laughed. He
was even a pretty decent ball player. At the time
I couldn't have told you any of that about him.
But looking back, this man of faith, who let some
kids use the church as a place to play, made a real
impression on me.

The minister of that small church was a simple man
of faith with a great heart who truly cared about
people. He took time to play with us neighborhood

kids in the churchyard, even if we didn't attend services there. He rolled up his sleeves and joined us, with a hearty laugh and a fast arm to first base. He often invited us to attend youth events at the church. Sometimes I went. One summer a neighbor invited me to go to a week of camp the church sponsored. My parents said yes, and I headed into New York's Finger Lakes region to a place that changed my life.

I gave my life to Christ at that week of camp. And when I came home I joined with the Christians to worship in that little church on my street. It wasn't long before my sister and parents started attending with me. We joined other families there on the journey of faith, all trying to follow Jesus the best we could. It was a community of grace.

When I was growing up, that church seemed very big to me, maybe because so much of my spiritual formation began there or because so many of the most important decisions of my life were made there. Or maybe it was because the people who started me on the spiritual journey were, in fact, giants of the faith.

There are thousands of churches like the one in Liverpool, New York, dotting the landscape of the world. They are communities of faith that make a difference in the lives of the people who play ball in the churchyard, come to know the kindhearted people inside, and commit themselves to traveling together on the spiritual journey. The next time you drive by the neighborhood church, maybe you ought to stop and go inside. It might just change your life.

 RICK RUSAW

Do you attend church? Why or why not? If you do, what brought you to your church? If you don't, what drove you away?

What would make you feel more accepted at church? What things might you do to help others feel welcomed?

Carry each other's burdens, and in this way you will fulfill the law of Christ.

GALATIANS 6:2

Stretcher

We could all use a friend like this, because he was nothing if not persistent.

Jesus was teaching in a house in the town of Capernaum. Crowds of people had gathered to hear him. You can picture the scene—people jammed in the living room, leaning in the windows, spilling out into the street. Rumor had already spread that Jesus not only had amazing things to say, but that he also was doing some amazing deeds. People who were blind, deaf, and suffering from other disabilities, were healed.

Now there was a man with a disability who had some very good friends. They knew if they could get their friend to Jesus, then just maybe he would walk again. No guarantees, no promises; but they believed that Jesus would do what they wanted him to do—try.

When they realized they couldn't even get close to the house, let alone see Jesus, they must have been disappointed. But at least one of these stretcher bearers wasn't about to be deterred.

Before you knew it, he and the disabled man were on top of the house; the friends were breaking through the hard clay of the rooftop and lowering their friend on his stretcher through the roof.

At this point, if you are the man on the stretcher, you must be asking yourself if this is really a good idea. You wonder if Jesus will toss you out or criticize your friends for their recklessness.

But before the man could utter an apology, Jesus commended the faithfulness of his friends and invited him to walk. You can only imagine how grateful the guy must have been for friends like that.

I can't help but read this story and be grateful for those who've carried the stretcher for me. It's likely someone has carried the stretcher for you too. It could have been a family member who prayed for you or a parent who took you to church. It may have been a friend whose example drew you closer to God.

If life has been at all good to you, you can be sure someone carried the stretcher for you. Drop that person a note or find another way to say thanks.

Then find a stretcher you can carry. You never know what will happen when you help someone meet Jesus.

RICK RUSAW

List the people who have "carried the stretcher" for you.
How did each of these people minister to you?

List the people you have helped carry. What did you do?
Who else in your life might need a stretcher bearer today?

Ever since I heard about your faith in the Lord Jesus and your love for all the saints, I have not stopped giving thanks for you, remembering you in my prayers.

EPHESIANS 1:15, 16

Someone Pays a Price

When I was in my twenties, more than one set of relieved parents called or wrote to thank me for being there for their wayward child. I was working with a Christian youth organization called Christ In Youth at the time, and I thought I was just doing my job.

I had no idea how deeply those parents felt their words of thanks.

My own children are now in their twenties. All
three are doing quite well. But the teen years were
not always fun. We'll leave it at that.

For a very long time, I thought if you did a good job
as a parent, you had nothing to worry about when
it came to the choices your children made. I was
quick to judge those parents whose children sowed
wild oats by the bushel. I was wrong. The children
of very good parents do not always make very good
decisions.

I now have a far greater appreciation for those
who are at the right place at the right time, gently
guiding, cajoling, nurturing, and restoring young
people who have lost their way—an old friend, a
college professor, a children's church director,
a young couple in their first full-time ministry.
Those were some of the folks who were there for my
children, providing the same encouragement my

wife, Cathryn, and I provided to another generation 25 years ago. And I am profoundly grateful for the love they showed to Jonathan, Jael, and Jana.

None of us can survive on the faith of our parents. There comes a time when we have to face the unanswerable questions ourselves, and draw conclusions that will chart the course of our own lives. As we travel those turbulent waters, nothing is more important than our fellow travelers on the journey. Not those who *have* to be there, like Mom and Dad, but those who *choose* to be there—who choose to love because they see something in us worth loving.

John Shea, in his book *An Experience Named Spirit*, tells of an old nun with red tennis shoes who brought peace into the life of an incorrigible young man. No matter how hard he pushed her away, the old nun kept coming back, until finally the young man's tough exterior façade broke, and he allowed grace and mercy into his life for the first time. It seems the old nun with the red shoes had a knack for helping wayward boys. Years of such work took their toll—loving others is hard work. Shea says, "People do change, but someone always pays the price."

To the old nun with red tennis shoes, to the psychology professor at the Christian college, to the children's church director, to my old friend, and to the young couple in the new church, to all those who have paid the price so the faith of another may grow and flourish, I say a heartfelt "Thank you."

■■ PAUL S. WILLIAMS

List a few specific people who paid the price to help you change and grow in your faith. Write down your plan to thank them personally.

List a few people you know who need someone to help them grow right now. Write a prayer for each of them, asking God to send friends into their lives to help them grow—ask him to send you, if that is his will.

To love God with all your heart, with all your understanding and with all your strength, and to love your neighbor as yourself is more important than all burnt offerings and sacrifices.

Mark 12:33

Won't You Be My Neighbor?

A man had been robbed, beaten, and left half-dead by the roadside. This is how Jesus began the story of the Good Samaritan.

We don't know if the background of the thieves had any role in their crime. Were they uneducated? Did they come from poverty? Had they no religious training? Nothing about that is mentioned. We do know, however, that two educated, prosperous experts on the Scriptures, a priest and a Levite, saw the half-dead man on the side of the road.

For many years in Pittsburgh, Pennsylvania, there lived a man with a modern-day status equal to the priest or the Levite. His name was Dr. William Orr, an author, professor, and distinguished New Testament scholar. His knowledge of the Scriptures was unrivaled. Students came to his lectures in droves. And one day, in the dead of winter, Dr. Orr came to a man by the side of the road.

They came, they saw, and they kept walking. Both the priest and the Levite did nothing for the dying man by the roadside. "But a Samaritan, as he traveled, came where the man was; and when he saw him, he took pity on him" (Luke 10:33).

Dr. William Orr was "the most beloved professor" in the history of the institution where he served.

Yet it was not his knowledge of the Scriptures or
his interesting lectures that made him so loved.
Education is wonderful, but it doesn't make
one good.

On many cold winter afternoons, Dr. Orr came
back from his lunch freezing and without a coat.
It seems that whenever he was out, he made a point
of not just *seeing* the men and women by the side
of the road, but caring for them, even to his own
detriment. Upon his death in 1993, a facility
was created in his honor and that of his wife: the
William and Mildred Orr Compassionate Care
Center. And though the center has helped thousands of homeless and elderly, it's only the beginning of Dr. Orr's legacy.

In answer to the question "Who is my neighbor?"
Jesus indicated it was just about anybody you meet
who needs help.

In his lectures Pittsburgh professor William Orr defined the word *neighbor* many times with words. But the only meaning his students remember is when he defined it with actions. The word meant a great deal to one student in particular, Fred Rogers. For over three decades, when *Mister Rogers* invited us to be his "neighbor," he was simply repeating the invitation given to him by his coatless friend and favorite professor, Dr. William Orr.

GREG ALLEN

Would you give a needy person the coat off your back or
the shoes off your feet? Why or why not? Whom do you
see daily or weekly that is in need, physically, emotion-
ally, or spiritually?

What is stopping you from being a "Good Samaritan" to
these people? Write a prayer asking God to help you see
and take the opportunities he gives you to love others in
his name.

I know that my Redeemer lives,

   and that in the end he will stand upon the earth.

JOB 19:25

He Was Good with That

You might have heard of Job, whom God referred to as one of a kind—blameless. The Bible tells us God allowed Satan to test Job, and test him he did. Satan had all Job's property and possessions destroyed. But then his children were destroyed too.

That would do it for me. I'm afraid I'd be ready to abandon God if my children were taken from me the way that Job's were.

Job's reaction to this gravest of disasters was nothing like mine would have been. When he learned of the death of his children, he did tear his clothes, shave his head, and fall to the ground. But it's what he did on the ground that amazes me.

He worshiped! He said that he came into this world with nothing, and so he'd leave with nothing. The Lord had given the good things, and now the Lord himself had taken them away. Rather than questioning the God of the universe, Job praised him.

Job's disaster was not over. God allowed Satan to give Job terribly painful boils. Job hurt so badly that he broke pottery and used the sharp edges to scrape his wounds. That's when Job's wife spoke up. She told him to curse God and die. Job's friends were devastated and said nothing for a week, but finally they advised him to question God.

But Job didn't. As a matter of fact, he told his wife she was talking like a foolish woman and asked her why we should accept good from God, but not trouble. Job had lost everything but his life, and now that was hanging by a thread. Still he refused to take the counsel of those closest to him and abandon God. Why?

There are many who want to follow God and do so with great joy as long as life is going well. But then there are those few who follow God against all odds. They swim upstream while everyone else floats down. Job was such a man. He didn't question God. Why? Because Job knew that no matter what happened to him, God was still God—and Job was not. Job was good with that. He would trust God no matter what.

Trusting God does not stop my pain or tears when I suffer, but it does offer me peace and hope to believe that the God of Job is deserving of my full devotion. God asks me, as he asked Job, to be obedient even when I am utterly and completely confused, disheartened, and discouraged. It's hard. But it is what God wants me to do.

So what happened at the end of this story? Well, Job got everything back. Yes, that's right! God gave it all back—health, family, land, wealth—everything. Amazing, isn't it? And I guess that's the point. If you stick with God, your story will always have a fantastic ending.

■■ GREG ALLEN AND PAUL S. WILLIAMS

What are your thoughts when you read about Job? How do you think you would react if put in the same situation?

Why is God worthy of our trust and worship, even when things are going wrong? What does Job's story teach you about persevering in your friendship with God through hard times?

Encourage one another and build each other up.

1 THESSALONIANS 5:11

Jackie Robinson

When Jackie Robinson first broke the racial barrier in major league baseball, the response he got from other teams and his own teammates was decidedly minor league. Opponents intentionally tried to injure him. He wasn't allowed to eat with his own team and found himself isolated and lonely.

It's hard to imagine the tremendous pressure Jackie Robinson endured in that first season. Yet that first year Robinson was named Rookie of the Year, an award that still bears his name today.

Jackie Robinson helped the Dodgers to six National League pennants. He was a regular addition to the annual all-star lineup and was the first African-American inducted into baseball's Hall of Fame. How did he accomplish so much when his career began with such difficulty?

Robinson spoke of one particular incident that saved his career. During his inaugural season, he was having a particularly bad stretch. He was accustomed to the boos and slurs from opposing fans at other ball parks, but now he was getting them in waves from hometown fans at Ebbets Field. After making two errors at second base, the fans started in relentlessly with catcalls and jeers so loud you couldn't hear anything else. Robinson stood in his position, head down, shuffling his feet in the dirt.

Then something out of the ordinary happened.

Pee Wee Reese, the Dodgers' shortstop, one of the most respected players in the game, walked toward the second baseman, put his arm around Jackie Robinson, and remained there until, slowly, the stands were silent. When the jeers had stopped, Reese slapped Robinson on the back and returned to his position while the game resumed.

Robinson would later say, "That one arm around my shoulder probably saved my career."

Encouragement is powerful. Whether it is a word, a smile, a note, or an arm around the shoulder, there is tremendous power in a gesture of encouragement. It doesn't take thousands booing to discourage us. A single negative voice can steal the wind from our sails. But it can also be a single voice, or a single arm on the shoulder, that gives us hope.

Jackie Robinson graced the world's stage with his presence, his inspiration, and his steadfast spirit. Who knows if any of that would have happened if Pee Wee Reese had stayed at his shortstop position that day. But he didn't. He walked to second base and put his arm around a teammate. And that changed everything.

■■ RICK RUSAW

When have you felt isolated and alone? Who has been an encouragement to you when you felt that way? How?

Have you ever taken a risk and put your arm around someone's shoulder, even when everyone else was boo-ing that person? Who could use your support right now?

*Jesus said, "I have come that they may have life,
and have it to the full."*

Private Friend—
Public Enemy

It was 1945 near the end of World War II, and in
the jungles of Southeast Asia a small band of guer-
rilla fighters struggled to resist well-equipped and
highly trained Japanese troops. Their leader was
a young man who had lived in the United States
working as a busboy in the Parker House Hotel
in Boston. He had returned to his homeland in
Indochina with a passion for her independence.

But now, as he desperately tried to lead the resistance, he found himself near death due to severe malaria and dysentery. The story of his rescue surprised everyone.

A highly trained intelligence team of U.S. soldiers code-named "Deer" silently parachuted into the dense jungle of Southeast Asia. They were to extract this guerilla leader who had been fighting the Japanese. U.S. intelligence had learned that he was near death from disease.

After the mission succeeded and the fallen leader was nursed back to health, the leader provided intelligence to rescue downed American pilots in exchange for weapons and ammunition.

The team recommended continued support for the rebel leader after the war, but their report was ignored. The leader himself petitioned President

Truman for help in gaining Indochina's independence from the French. But his politics and tactics
were considered too controversial, and his requests
were denied.

In the end, this private friend of America would
quickly become one of our greatest public enemies.
His name was Ho Chi Minh.

Sixty thousand Americans died in Vietnam fighting
Communist forces led by Ho Chi Minh, this former
ally of the United States who, in World War II, was
spared certain death by a U.S. rescue team. A pho-
tograph shows him seated with smiling American
soldiers after his rescue and return to health.
They had given him his life . . . and he would use it
against them.

Sadly, I see people reacting the same way to God.
He has given us so much. Our very existence is his

gift to us. Perhaps you don't consider that much of a gift. You may be confused, angry, or even heart-broken. You could be at a point where you don't even think life is worth living.

Could it be you have received God's gift of life and are using it against him? Are you thinking of yourself as his friend, but living as his enemy? It doesn't have to be that way. When we offer ourselves in honor to him and seek God as a friend, he promises to stand by us forever.

Life itself is God's gift to you. What you do with it is your gift to God.

When was the last time you thanked God for the gift of life he has given you? Take time and thank God for the blessing of life. How can your life be a gift to God today?

What act of service, kind word, or offering of praise can you give? Write a prayer, asking the Lord to show you how your life can be a blessing to him and to those around you.

Let us not give up meeting together, as some are in the habit of doing, but let us encourage one another.

HEBREWS 10:25

Alone to the Bone

The construction workers in Tokyo, Japan, were making their last rounds in a decrepit building slated for demolition. They could not have been prepared for what they found.

With a passing glance, one of the workers happened to see a door to an apartment long forgotten. What they discovered inside was enough to stun and bewilder anyone.

A human skeleton wearing pajamas was seated on a small couch with a newspaper, dated February 20, 1984, lying open on its lap. The man, a construction worker himself, had died 20 years previously . . . and nobody knew it.

His family never missed him. No coworkers came calling. An elderly neighbor living in the same building said he didn't even know the apartment was there. I call that being "alone to the bone."

How can a person be that alone?

Honestly, I don't think it would be that difficult. Simply shut yourself off from the rest of the world. Be preoccupied with your own existence. Concentrate on your loneliness. Feed your resentment. Ignore others. Neglect family. People will have no problem forgetting you. Who could blame them?

If we are feeling lonely, neglected, or forgotten, perhaps we do bear some responsibility for it. When a man has been dead for all of 20 years and nobody takes note, it has to say something about his unwillingness to share his life with anyone!

If you are alone, I don't mean to belittle your circumstances. Loneliness is brutal.

But listen carefully. You are the only one who can do anything about it. If you are able to dial a phone or pick up a pen and paper, then you don't have to be alone.

Take the initiative to connect with others. Extend best wishes to a young couple expecting their first child. Call your grandson on the phone and tell him you'll be praying for him as he begins college.

Those we bless will gladly become our companions. No matter our location, age, or station in life, what we give to others, even the simplest of gifts, will always come back and nourish us.

What do you do when you're feeling lonely?
When do you feel most alone?

Who should you reach out and connect with today?
Write down some names and make an effort to reach out
to those people today.

It is for freedom that Christ has set us free.

GALATIANS 5:1

Freedom Through Obedience

I am, without apology, one of those who would call himself a dog person.

I haven't been without of a dog for most of my adult life. And I have no intention of changing that fact. My current canine companion is a very large, very white, very lovable character named Kodi who accompanies me almost everywhere.

Over the years I've noticed something about dogs. They can be conveniently lumped into three categories. There are dogs that run wild in the streets. They're wary, often dangerous, and left to fend for themselves. Then there are companion dogs that must be kept on a leash for fear of running away. They are well cared for but their boundaries are necessarily tight. Finally, there are those dogs whose owners have invested significant time and effort in training them. They walk off-leash, alert and eager to respond to the commands of their masters.

I have a good friend whose golden retriever accompanies her to the coffee shop. The dog has been trained to sit at the door outside and wait until his master comes back. Because this beautiful dog has been trained so well, owner and dog can go just about anywhere together, to the point of even crossing busy streets with no need for a leash.

There's a life lesson to be found here. Freedom comes through obedience.

The relationship between a well-trained dog and its owner is always a beautiful thing to observe. The animal experiences genuine freedom. There is mutual respect and affection that touches us. Such sophisticated training is almost always for a specific purpose whereby dog and owner can serve each other. It is through unqualified obedience that a dog finds freedom, purpose, and the loving care of its master.

Am I getting to you here? Are we tuning in to the profound lesson provided by our canine companions?

There are really only two options for how to live your life. You can live it your way or God's way. Here's how Paul puts it in Galatians 5:16, 17:

"Live freely, animated and motivated by God's Spirit. Then you won't feed the compulsions of selfishness. For there is a root of sinful self-interest in us that is at odds with a free spirit, just as the free spirit is incompatible with selfishness" *(The Message)*.

You can insist on attempting to make life submit to your rules and be enslaved by it, or you can obey God's plan for you and discover freedom like you've never known, a freedom that carries a sense of purpose, joy, and a loving relationship with the master.

What are your thoughts about the idea of freedom through obedience? Are there other examples that show you the truth of this concept?

When have you experienced the freedom that comes with obedience? When have you gone your own way and lost freedom? What did these experiences teach you about how you should live your life?

I will listen to what God the LORD will say;

    he promises peace to his people, his saints.

PSALM 85:8

On Being Still

Henri Nouwen has taught me much about being
still and quiet. One of my favorite books is based
on some of Nouwen's graduate students' studies on
the Desert Fathers. The Desert Fathers were monks
who chose to pursue God by withdrawing from the
noise of the world and retreating to the desert to
spend time reading and listening and then writing
about their understanding of a relationship with
the creator. Nouwen's grad students read the writ-

ten works of these desert monks and noticed three
common themes—silence, solitude, and prayer.

According to the Desert Fathers, silence is more
than just being quiet; it is finding a place where
silence is uninterrupted. That explains why they
retreated to the desert. Solitude is being totally
alone; no friends, no family, no golden retriever.
And the Fathers defined prayer as *listening* to God
rather than *talking* to God. They spoke with him,
but they preferred listening.

The day I took their advice and found a place where
I was alone and quiet so I could listen is a day I long
to repeat. The first few hours of awkward silence
were followed by peaceful bliss. And I was shocked
by how much I heard in the deafening silence.

I'm most comfortable when I'm busy and checking off task lists. So was Martha. When Martha

opened her home to Jesus and his disciples, she immediately busied herself with household tasks. But Martha's sister did just the opposite. She did nothing except sit close to Jesus and listen to what he said. Martha was furious. Like me, Martha felt that greater productivity was born out of physical action. And with so much to do, she wondered, *How could anyone waste time by just sitting and listening?*

Jesus wasn't a Desert Father, but he spoke out of his desert experience. Productivity is not necessarily the result of being busy. We may feel better about ourselves by checking off a to-do list, but is our "self" any better off?

Jesus told Martha that her sister Mary had chosen the most productive action plan, so I want to follow that same plan. I want to improve my skills of sitting and listening.

When I worship God, I notice a war within me. I fight the urge to stay busy rather than take a few minutes to be quiet. I'm not very good at listening. I'm great with task lists, but I need to improve my skill of being still. I'd like to honor my friends by being a better listener. I'd like to honor my God by being a better listener, especially as I know he is listening to me. I have the sense that my productivity would skyrocket if I would intentionally slow down, be quiet, and listen to God. Perhaps today will be your best opportunity to do nothing—except to make the most of it, and just be still.

■ Greg Allen

What are your feelings about taking a day off just for silence, solitude, and prayer—a day spent just with God? What might you gain from doing "nothing" for a day?

Rate yourself as a listener. Do you really hear what people say to you or are you more concerned with how you will respond? Have you taken time to listen to God lately? What is he saying to you?

Even in darkness light dawns for the upright,

    for the gracious and compassionate and righteous man.

PSALM 112:4

A Righteous Man

I have a friend whose background is very different from mine. He grew up in a major Eastern city,
spoke a foreign language, and attended a Catholic
university. I grew up in the suburban Midwest and
attended a Bible college. I'm a minister. He's a
physician. I talk a lot. He's soft-spoken and shy.

But over 20 years ago our paths crossed, and in
spite of our differences, a friendship developed.

I am richer for that experience. My friend is extraordinarily even and steady and always attuned to the needs of others, be it his family, his patients, or his neighbors. In fact, the word I'd use to describe him is a word not well understood or often used today. That word is *righteous*.

It seems today, whenever we use the word *righteous*, it's always in a negative connotation, usually with the word *self* attached to it. As in, "What a self-righteous jerk that guy is"—referring to those who feel divinely appointed to make us aware of our shortcomings. You're probably picturing someone right now.

But lost in our frustration with self-righteousness is the healthy meaning of the term *righteous*. One of my favorite writers, Barbara Brown Taylor, says a righteous person is one whose aim is true. That defines my friend perfectly. While he may not hit the mark every time (he's human just like the rest of us), his aim is always true. And if you spend much time with him, you see he is a righteous man.

The term *righteous* is not a negative term. A righteous person is quite simply one who follows God's commands. Righteousness is about doing what you know is right, whether you feel like it or not. It's about the practice of faith, not the feeling of faith.

I remember one time I thought I was dying in the middle of the night. This physician friend met me at his office and determined I had nothing more than a simple virus. I was unbelievably embarrassed, but he reassured me that I did the right thing by calling him (like he really wanted to get up in the middle of the night). That's what I mean when I say he is righteous. He goes beyond what you'd expect. His aim is true.

My friend doesn't wear his faith on his sleeve. He doesn't talk about loving others. He loves others. He doesn't talk about serving God. He serves God. His actions speak loud and clear. And that is the essence of a righteous man.

PAUL S. WILLIAMS

Do you know someone you would consider righteous according to God's definition? What qualities make that person righteous?

Would people say you are righteous? Why or why not? What might need to change in your life to make you a more righteous person in the eyes of God and others?

Let us . . . approach the throne of grace with confidence,
so that we may receive mercy and find grace to help us in our time
of need.

HEBREWS 4:16

Prayer

During my years in ministry, I've heard many kinds
of prayers. For instance, there's the announce-
ment prayer: "God, thank you for the church picnic
this Sunday at 2:00, and please remind everyone to
bring a dish to share."

Or there's the guilt trip prayer: "Lord, you know
we only need 10 more workers for our children's
department, and there are 20 people here today

who haven't volunteered for anything since the world was created. Please convict them right now with the need to serve!"

And then there's the saddest of all, the gossip prayer: "We know our dear brother Bob has sinned before all, but we must learn to forgive."

Of course, none of those are what God had in mind when he told us to pray. He intended for prayer to be something quite different.

I looked up the word *prayer* on the Internet recently, and the results amazed me. One Web site offered software kits for five of the major world religions. Just install, read the instruction manual to select the god of your choice, and then start praying.

I saw sites for Buddhist digital prayer wheels, spiritual herbs, prayer in schools, no prayer in schools, prayer flags, prayer walks, prayer stones. It all seems so complicated.

And it's so very different from Jesus' simple words: "Come to me, all you who are weary and burdened, and I will give you rest" (Matthew 11:28).

Jesus doesn't say, "Come to me when you have it all figured out." He doesn't say, "Come to me if you agree with every word in the Bible." He doesn't even say, "Come to me if you're sure you believe."

He says simply, "Come."

Sometimes it's easy to think that God is hard to reach. And yet the Bible tells us we have a direct line to God—no voice mail, no waiting in line, and no one taking messages. I may not be able to talk to the rich and powerful on earth, but I have direct access to the creator of the universe. The book of

Hebrews tells us to walk right up—without hesitation—into the very presence of God.

There was a 4-year-old who listened to the Lord's Prayer each Sunday in church and tried to say it along with his parents. One Sunday as the church recited the familiar words, the little boy could be heard above the others praying loudly, "Our Father, who art in Heaven, I know you know my name."

Out of the mouths of babes . . .

God does know *your* name, and he simply invites you to come.

■■ Jen Taylor for Greg Allen

What does prayer mean to you?
What do you say and do when you pray?

How does it make you feel to know that the God of the universe knows you by name? How could this concept change your prayer life?

[Jesus said,] "I tell you the truth, whatever you did for one of the least of these brothers of mine, you did for me."

MATTHEW 25:40

Simple Visits

I know of a quaint home located in a fairly large city. It is a retirement home and one of the residents is Verlin. Verlin is 90 years old. His wife died a year ago, but Verlin doesn't seem lonely. He has several regular visitors including extended family and many friends. But there is one particular guest who brightens that quaint home more than all the others. He is a 71-year-old friend named Royce. Royce and Verlin discuss computers, family, and history—the visits give Verlin a sense of honor, dignity, and encouragement. But I'm guessing the favorite topic of Royce's visit is the 28 years of mentorship the two have shared. In earlier years Royce learned much from Verlin about being a husband, a father, a good employee, and a good friend. But mostly Verlin taught Royce about friendship with God. And in these final years, Royce's gratitude is expressed to Verlin through these simple visits.

It's hard to be a child, or the parent of a child, spending Christmas with doctors and medicine instead of with family and presents. One Christmas at a particular children's hospital, families began to hear singing in the hallway. Several teenagers had decided to think more of others than of themselves, so they roamed the corridors of a hospital to bring a bit of Christmas cheer to a few children. These children had leukemia, fevers, broken arms, and broken hearts . . . but for a moment their imaginations were carried away to a snowy night filled with lights and reindeer. Just for a moment they could smile, and all because of a simple visit.

When Edna was married to Fred, she lived in a simple but comfortable home in a regular Midwestern town. After her husband died and she suffered a stroke, Edna moved in with her daughter Marilyn. Caring for Edna was a full-time job, but Melsa made the job easier with simple visits. Melsa would come by almost every day and help Edna change from pajamas to day clothes, feed her a meal, and make lively conversation.

I don't know who benefited most from the visits, Edna or Marilyn or maybe even Melsa. There were no scientific discoveries or great business deals made when the three ladies were together. But Edna was honored, Marilyn encouraged, and Melsa invigorated by those simple visits where the greatest gift of all was shared . . . love and care for one another.

These are three simple stories, but they show the incredible impact one person can have by taking the time to visit another. This is truly what makes the world a better place.

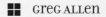 GreG ALLen

When has a simple visit from friends or family lifted your spirits? When someone takes time out of his or her busy life to spend time with you and show you love, how does it make you feel?

To whom can you pay a simple visit today? How might your kind action make the world a better place? Write down your ideas.

If I rise on the wings of the dawn,
> *if I settle on the far side of the sea,*
even there your hand will guide me, LORD,
> *your right hand will hold me fast.*

PSALM 139:9, 10

Hide-and-Seek

"I can do it all by myself." I remember when each of my children first spoke those words. It was the day I realized the apple hadn't fallen far from the tree. For too long I had taken pride in my self-sufficiency and my ability to handle life on my own. Rugged individualism is the great American way. We seem to think somehow we are strong when we manage life alone. Yet it is that very attitude that can leave us vulnerable to attack.

In my neighborhood growing up, playing hide-and-seek was a nightly summer ritual. Nearly all the neighborhood kids would play. There was Mark, who never wanted to hide alone, and Melanie, who hid in the same place every time. Some were good hiders, and some were good seekers. But no one could hold a candle to Larry.

Larry was great at hiding. In fact, he was so good that we didn't spend much time looking for him. Almost always there would be a long argument with him about not playing fairly. But still Larry would hide and hide and hide. He was so good at hiding that if you were to go to my childhood neighborhood today, you might still find him hiding there!

Throughout my life I have spent time hiding, not wanting to be found, and I have friends who have hidden too. Russ didn't tell his kids about his bad heart until it was too late for them to say goodbye. Michelle wouldn't tell her friends about her depression and traveled that road too long by herself. Roger hid his company's financial trouble from his family until he took his own life.

Sometimes we hide too well. "I can do it all by myself. I don't need anybody." The problem with that philosophy is that we were never created to tackle life alone. We all need help on the journey.

Each of my three children liked playing hide-and-seek when they were young. I hate to admit this, but my daughter Chelsea wasn't very good at the game. She would hide in the same place every time—in her closet behind the laundry basket. I would start out in the garage. "Is Chelsea hiding in the recycle bin?" Then it was on to the kitchen. "Is Chelsea hiding in the freezer?" The giggles would start coming from her room. Then I would head into my bedroom. "Is she hiding in the closet?"

Before I could get to her room, she would come running down the hall and jump into my arms.

The point of the game for Chelsea wasn't hiding, it was being found. The joy wasn't seeing how long it would take for me to find her, but how quickly we could be reconnected to each other. Chelsea is older now, and, unfortunately, she is learning to hide better. I'm hoping I can always help her remember the real joy is in being found.

 RICK RUSAW

Why do people hide things—their hurts, struggles, failures? What is the worst that could happen if we stopped hiding and admitted these things? What is the best that could happen?

What are you hiding from today?
Are you ready to be found? Why or why not?

You did not receive a spirit that makes you a slave again to fear, but you received the Spirit of sonship. And by him we cry, "Abba, Father." The Spirit himself testifies with our spirit that we are God's children.

ROMANS 8:15, 16

All in a Name

I have an ordinary name—a bit too ordinary unfortunately. I recently read that Williams is the third most common name in America, even more common than Brown or Jones. Nobody ever asks how to spell Williams. Everyone knows. And Paul? There's one on every block.

The Paul Williams with whom I'm compared most often is the pop music composer and performer of the 1970s. I never did much care for his voice, though I was partial to his tunes. He composed a number of hits for The Carpenters among others and managed to become a regular of sorts on the talk show circuit.

That Paul Williams hasn't been seen on television in well over a decade, but my fellow Baby Boomers remember him well. I walk up to the airline counter and the agent invariably says, "Hey, you're a lot taller and not as blond as I remember."

The agent is proud of himself. He doesn't realize I've heard that joke 832 times before. I try to be gracious and give the agent some return on his clever investment.

Paul Williams is who I am. It is my name. It's me. I come from a long line of Williamses; and on a spring afternoon in the early 1950s in Huntington,

West Virginia, my parents told the hospital staff my name would be Paul. And so it is.

We adopted our daughter from India when she was 2 months of age, and we gave her the Hebrew name Jael. We liked that the name meant "divine surprise," since she was our surprise gift from God. Unfortunately, the only time the name appears in the Bible is when Jael drives a tent peg through a sleeping king's head!

When Jael was a teen, she read that story in the book of Judges. She came into the family room afterwards.

"So, Dad, you take an Indian child with brown skin, bring her into a white American family, and give her the Hebrew name of a woman who drove a spike through a king's head. Thanks a lot." Then she left the room.

What were we thinking? If we had to stick with *J*
names, then a good Indian name like Jubi, or an
American name like Jennifer would have been fine.
But no, we had to give her a name you can never
find on a refrigerator magnet. Fortunately, she's a
kindhearted person who forgave us long ago. She
still has the name though.

God wants us to know his name, even though we
often don't honor it as we should. As Frederick
Buechner writes, God went and named himself and
hasn't had a minute's peace since. Still, it is good
to have a God who wants us to call him by name and
speak to him whenever our hearts desire. He actually
invites us to call him Abba—which is also a Hebrew
name. It means "daddy." Like a loving daddy, God
promises to always listen, and he never stops loving
us. God is the name we can trust, always.

 PAUL S. WILLIAMS

What does your name mean or signify?
Is it meaningful to you or would you like it to be something else?

What does it mean to you that God wants you to call him Daddy? What do you need to ask from your Daddy in Heaven today? He's waiting to hear and listen.

Wisdom is found in those who take advice.

PROVERBS 13:10

Wise Counsel

If you need some advice, don't come to me. I make decisions quickly—like right now—without taking long to weigh the evidence, consider the facts, or make a list of pros and cons. I'll be happy to make a decision for you—but it'll be my decision, not yours.

While I'm not very good at giving advice, I do often seek it. I don't look for people who make my decisions for me or who give me quick solutions before I've even explained the problem. I look for trusted and wise friends who will listen carefully before they speak.

About 15 years ago I was considering a job change. I was advised to seek the counsel of trusted friends who have a track record of making good personal decisions.

I sought advice from Ross and Eugene. I trusted them, and they cared enough to listen to the pros and cons. They spent a couple hours asking questions and listening to my answers. Those two hours raised even more questions in my mind. Still undecided, I realized that patience was called for.

As I contemplated the advice of my friends, I realized they were pointing me to God and to his Word for my answers. In the book of James, the Bible says wisdom is ours for the asking. So I prayed daily to God for guidance and direction. I asked for wisdom, I read the Bible, and I waited.

A day gave way to a week and then a month and then three months. After three months of waiting, there were still unanswered questions, but for the most part I found something I hadn't felt in quite some time—peace.

I knew what I needed to do. The advice of my friends and the wisdom gained through patience led me to a decision. I turned down the job. It's a decision I do not regret.

Big decisions often require big chunks of time. When I rush into decision-making, I forfeit peace and make poor choices. But when I practice patience, my stress level lessens and wise counsel bubbles up.

If you are facing a big decision, seek wise counsel, be patient, read the Word of God, and pray. Following these steps will lead you down the path to the right choice—and to peace.

■ GREG ALLEN

In what areas of your life do you need to learn to have more patience? What decisions are you prone to rush into?

List some friends who have a track record of making good personal decisions. How might you further cultivate these relationships and learn from these wise friends?

No discipline seems pleasant at the time, but painful. Later on, however, it produces a harvest of righteousness and peace for those who have been trained by it.

Making Decisions— Dad, Daughter, and God

I have read about it and heard about it, but it has finally happened to me. I have entered the realm of the ignorant. And it's my high school age daughter who has ushered me into this realm of the unknowing. She's done it through phrases like these: "Are you kidding, Dad?" and "Don't you know anything?" and "Well, *everybody* knows that."

We are experiencing the age-old collision of parent and teen over the issues of freedom and values. What I've tried to share with my wonderful daughter is that Daddy has already lived through all her questions and can give her the answers if she'd only ask. But I've discovered she doesn't ask the questions because, you see, she already *knows* the answers.

I can't pick on my teenage daughter too much because I remember being a freshman in high school and believing my parents were among the least knowledgeable humans on planet Earth. Sure, my dad would tell me he'd "been there, done that," but I wasn't interested in his past—only my future. I remember Dad telling me to be extremely careful with the car, yet I ignored his advice and got a traffic ticket shortly after getting my license.

Dad taught me about even more important matters too, like not getting too serious with just one girl too early, and never being in a house alone with a girl. I heeded his advice on these issues, and I'm glad I did. As I look back, I now realize I didn't have nearly as many answers as I thought I had. Now, if I can only get my own teenage daughter to believe that.

It is humorous to watch my daughter repeat to me the things I said to my own father. I doubted his wisdom, did not trust his advice, dismissed his counsel as uninformed, and classified all his thinking as from "the olden days." Now I know that what goes around, comes around!

What I want to avoid is having my heavenly Father experience the same thing with me. He has given marvelous counsel through the Bible. I never want to dismiss his words as uninformed or out of date. Many people do, disregarding God's teachings, claiming we live in a new day. I think we would disagree if our children tried that logic with us. So I choose to enjoy being the father of a teenager— and also being a child whose heavenly Father will always have advice worth following.

■■ GREG ALLEN

What life lessons did you learn from your parents?
How has your perspective changed about your parents
and the wisdom they offered in your youth?

What about your heavenly Father—what have you
learned from him? How has your perspective on his
wisdom changed as you've grown in your relationship
with him?

Plans fail for lack of counsel,

but with many advisers they succeed.

proverbs 15:22

The Value of a Mentor

Tiger Woods. Michael Jordan. Hank Aaron. Johnny
Unitas. What did they all have in common? The
answer I'm looking for is not "they all play a sport."
The common denominator is that these great ath-
letes all had coaches—mentors, to help them hone
their skills. Great business leaders, artists, minis-
ters, teachers, and people of all walks of life need
coaches. Mentors have acquired much wisdom
through experience and can pass that on to you.

There are any number of parents who could ben-
efit from finding a mentor who could coach them
through their children's "terrible twos," the begin-
nings of adolescent rebellion, the onset of the
teenage years, and the changing relationships with
adult children. Rather than go it alone, my wife and
I have sought the advice of several experienced and
successful parents.

In addition to great advice, we received empa-
thy from these seasoned parents, along with the
encouraging words "You'll be fine, you'll see." I
don't know that my wife and I were always "fine,"
but we were less stressed knowing our mentors had
been there before, and survived.

Mentors can help with finances too. There are
some simple and honorable tips about stewardship
that you could learn from financial mentors. I
was once encouraged to give God 10 percent, save

10 percent, and live off the rest. Another advised me to start children out early with separate little piggy banks to teach them what to give away, what to keep, and what to spend. We should take advantage of this counsel and learn to make money work for us so that we don't find ourselves working for the money.

Mentors are great for help with parenting and money, and many other everyday issues. But the mentors I value most are the ones I look to for spiritual growth. These great mentors don't even have to know my name, but I know them. I know them first and foremost by their lifestyles. I watch them interact with God and others, watch their stress levels; I notice their responses to tragedy, wealth, children, and controversy. I'll ask an occasional question of those who mentor me personally, and I'll pay special attention to the tone, the heart, and the spirit of their answers.

I am blessed with many mentors in my life. They always speak of God more than of themselves. Some are wealthy and some not so wealthy, but they are always grateful to God for his provision in their life. As for me, I will be eternally grateful that God has placed them in my path, and I pray I will always heed the wise advice they bring to my journey.

■ GREG ALLEN

Have you had mentors throughout your life?
If you have, how have they influenced who you are today?

If you haven't had a mentor, why not? Pray and ask God to bring someone to mind that you should ask to be your mentor. Maybe you are in a position to be able to offer wisdom from your life experiences to someone in need. Who comes to mind that could use your words of wisdom and gentle guidance?

Everyone should be quick to listen, slow to speak and slow to become angry.

james 1:19

I Was So Sure I Was Right

My cousin Martha loves her hometown of Grayson, Kentucky. Grayson is nestled in the foothills of the eastern part of the commonwealth, about 30 miles south of Ohio and 30 miles west of West Virginia. Grayson's not known for much in particular, but like many similar towns, it has a way about it. My mother spent her high school and college years there, and her oldest sister spent most of her life in Grayson. When I was a child, we visited often.

During one summer visit when I was about 12, Martha said she was going to live in this exact spot for the rest of her life. I told her that wasn't likely, since most people grow up and move out of their parents' houses. I was quite sure I was right.

Well, somewhere after the "move out" part of my reply, Martha put her hands over her ears and started singing loudly. The more I talked, the louder she sang. Martha's commitment to her particular vision of the future was sacred, and no cousin from Ohio was going to change her mind.

In the winter of 2003, I listened as two airplane passengers carried on a loud debate about the war with Iraq. What began as a friendly discussion ended as a verbal row that brought the flight attendant out from the galley. Both men were nearly shouting, and they may as well have been covering their ears with their hands.

The conflict in Iraq brought more passion about America's involvement in a war than I'd seen since Vietnam. But most debates, interviews, and protests seemed to be lacking one thing—respect for those holding an opposing view. With a plethora of talk shows desperate for ratings, rhetoric flew and passions were fanned, while both sides marched to polar extremes, hands over ears, singing loudly.

A few months before the Iraq War, a minister I deeply respect confided to a small group that the older he becomes, the more he respects the arguments for pacifism. Another participant said his Eastern European friends remember well the recent tyranny of the Soviet Union, and the price to be paid when totalitarianism isn't stopped. I spoke up about Dietrich Bonhoeffer's struggle over whether or not to participate in the plot to assassinate Hitler. Was it a noble decision or a misguided response incompatible with his Christian faith?

Our discussion continued for quite some time.

The world needs healthy give-and-take conversations—not hands over the ears and loud singing. We need to realize that tough issues should
be discussed among neighbors with respect and
openness. How else can we find a redemptive way
through so many shades of gray?

By the way, Martha still lives on Landsdowne
Avenue in Grayson, Kentucky, in the exact spot
where she lived when I was 12. But I was so sure I
was right. . . .

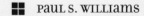 PAUL S. WILLIAMS

How do you listen to people who have views that oppose your own? Do you really listen and try to understand their points of view, or are you formulating your response and waiting for your chance to argue?

How would our families, churches, and nations be different if we adopted open and respectful dialogue as our way of bringing resolution to every issue? What can you do to reinforce this way of communicating in your own conversations?

"You will seek me and find me when you seek me with all your heart. I will be found by you," declares the Lord.

JEREMIAH 29:13, 14

Dodgeball

It was a childhood playground game, often the staple activity of middle school gym class—dodgeball.

The game is as simple as the name implies. People from one team throw balls at people on another team. The point is to avoid getting hit at all costs while attempting to hit others. When you get hit, you are out. The team of the last one standing wins!

Dodgeball was very popular until the late 1970s when those with authority decided it was harmful to a child's psyche. No more dodgeball.

Today the game is coming back with amazing popularity. No longer the childhood game of our adolescent years—now there are adult dodgeball leagues and tournaments popping up everywhere. Grown men and women are throwing balls, getting hit, and doing their best to dodge the ball.

Perhaps it's a revolt against authoritarian thinking, maybe it is just a new craze in aerobic exercise, or maybe it is just fun. Dodgeball is a simple game that is actually a pretty good metaphor for life.

You line up, work hard to avoid getting hit, take your lumps when they come, and the last one standing wins. But then the whistle blows. There is another game, and the outcome rarely remains the same.

No one can dodge the ball forever.

Some of us, though, have learned the lessons of dodgeball all too well. We dodge responsibility, discipline, tough circumstances, difficult decisions, and a long list of other elements of life—things that author M. Scott Peck called "legitimate suffering."

Worse yet, often we dodge God.

Content to see others whose faith sustains them, we promise ourselves that someday we will figure this God thing all out. Until then, we will just keep dodging, trying to stay out of the way of making any real decisions.

The majestic creator of the universe has invited us to pursue him, to seek him . . . and if we do, he won't "dodge" us.

If we quit dodging God, we might find the very thing we have been looking for—and come out winners in the end.

RICK RUSAW

Reflect back on when you played dodgeball or a similar game. Were you one of the risk takers, or were you terrified of getting hit and looking for the quickest way of escape? Do you see a reflection of how you live your life today in how you played when you were a child?

If you are dodging God, what are you most afraid of? If you are pursuing him, what are you discovering in your search?

Let the morning bring me word of your unfailing love,

   for I have put my trust in you.

Show me the way I should go,

   for to you I lift up my soul.

PSALM 143:8

What Follows

After he had risen from the dead, Jesus made several appearances.

Once while some of his disciples were fishing on the Sea of Galilee, he appeared on the shore. He was cooking some breakfast over a fire. When Peter saw Jesus, he jumped out of the boat and swam to him. When they had finished eating, Jesus asked Peter three questions. Actually, it was the same question three times. "Peter, do you love me?" he said. "If you do, take care of my sheep." And then he made this statement, "Peter, follow me."

Jesus didn't say where to follow him or where the path was going. He just said, "Follow me." Peter turned around to see that the disciple John was behind them. "What about John?" Peter asked Jesus. "Aren't you interested in him?"

And Jesus, in essence, said, "If I wanted to talk to him, I would have asked for him. But I'm talking to you. *You*, Peter, follow me" (From John 21:15-24).

I never planned on going into the ministry—it's not what I wanted to do. I grew up in New York and planned to go into business. I never really wanted to live in the South, and yet I ended up being an associate minister in Fort Myers, Florida. I never desired to do college administration in

the Midwest, but I ended up being an administra-
tor at a college in Cincinnati. And I never thought
I would live in Colorado, but now I'm a minister
in a church there. That's not what I wanted to do.
But I'm learning, through hindsight and through
the guidance of the Bible, that God knows what I
should be doing.

Following God isn't always easy. Sometimes the
road is unfamiliar with sharp turns. Finding direction can be complicated. There have been times I
wished God would just tell me what he wants me to
do—give me some kind of handwriting on the wall
or a postcard in the mail. But it hasn't happened
that way.

When I am unsettled about how things are going in
my life, I want to turn around and ask, "Lord, what
about these other people? Don't you want them to
go the same way I am going?" And then I remember

Peter, and I find myself on the shore of the Sea of Galilee. And from across the fire, Jesus looks up at me and says, "Rick, *you* follow me. Follow me. Trust me."

■ RICK RUSAW

In what areas of your life are you seeking God's guidance and direction? Do you hesitate to give your life over to God, fearing that his call for your life would be the last thing you want to do?

We all can learn from the disciples who dropped everything and followed Jesus. Do you long for that kind of faith and trust? Write a prayer asking God to give you the faith to trust him more and more each day.